Cloud Data Warehousing

2nd Snowflake Special Edition

by Joe Kraynak and David Baum

A Wiley Brand

Cloud Data Warehousing For Dummies®, 2nd Snowflake Special Edition

Published by
John Wiley & Sons, Inc.
111 River St.
Hoboken, NJ 07030-5774
www.wiley.com

For general information on our other products and services, or how to create a custom For Dummies book for your business or organization, please contact our Business Development Department in the U.S. at 877-409-4177, contact info@dummies.biz, or visit www.wiley.com/go/custompub. For information about licensing the For Dummies brand for products or services, contact BrandedRights&Licenses@Wiley.com.

ISBN 978-1-119-66647-9 (pbk); 978-1-119-66651-6 (ebk)

Manufactured in the United States of America

C10014347_101019

Publisher's Acknowledgments

We're proud of this book and of the people who worked on it. For details on how to create a custom For Dummies book for your business or organization, contact info@dummies.biz or visit www.wiley.com/go/custompub. For details on licensing the For Dummies brand for products or services, contact BrandedRights&Licenses@Wiley.com.

Some of the people who helped bring this book to market include the following:

Development Editor: Nicole Sholly

Project Editor: Martin V. Minner

Executive Editor: Steve Hayes

Editorial Manager: Rev Mengle

Business Development Representative: Karen Hattan

Production Editor: Mohammed Zafar Ali

Snowflake Contributors Team: Vincent Morello, Clarke Patterson, Leslie Steere, Kent Graziano

Table of Contents

Introduction

As an executive, manager, or analyst, you're well aware that knowledge is power and that data properly analyzed on a timely basis provides the insight necessary to make well-informed decisions and achieve a competitive advantage. Today, organizations have a much greater collection of more relevant data than ever before. This includes a diverse range of sources, internal and external, including data marts, cloud-based applications, and machine-generated data.

Unfortunately, the data warehouse architecture of the past 30 years continues to strain under the burden of extremely large, diverse data sets. Analysts often wait 24 hours or more for data to flow into the data warehouse before it's available for analysis. They can wait even longer for complex queries to run on that data. In many cases, the storage and compute resources required to process and analyze that data are insufficient. This leads to systems hanging or crashing. To avoid this, users and workloads must be queued, which results in even longer delays. In more recent times, alternative approaches have emerged, such as varying forms of the data lake. Yet, these solutions have brought their own limitations.

To remain efficient and competitive, organizations must be able to harness the power of the vast amounts of data constantly being generated and conduct complex analysis on that data. Fortunately, the commercialization of cloud computing emerged more than ten years ago and offers advances in computer hardware, architecture, and software that can help your organization meet this challenge and exceed your expectations.

About This Book

Welcome to the second edition of *Cloud Data Warehousing For Dummies*, where you discover how your organization can tap the power of massive amounts of data conveniently and affordably to enhance efficiency and transform raw data into valuable business intelligence.

More data opens the door to more and bigger opportunities, which are almost always accompanied by equally big challenges. To take advantage of these big opportunities, you need to implement a data warehouse solution that can store and organize data in diverse formats, provide convenient access to it, and improve the speed at which you can analyze it. And it must be done as cost-effectively as possible. This book shows you how.

Icons Used in This Book

Throughout this book, the following icons highlight tips, important points to remember, and more:

TIP

Tips guide you to easier ways to perform a task or better ways to use cloud data warehousing in your organization.

REMEMBER

This icon highlights concepts worth remembering as you immerse yourself in the understanding and application of cloud data warehousing.

CASE STUDY

The case studies in this book reveal how those organizations applied cloud data warehousing to save money and significantly improve the speed and performance of their data analytics.

Beyond the Book

If you like what you read in this book and want to know more, we invite you to visit www.snowflake.com, where you can find out more about the company and what it offers, trial Snowflake for free, obtain details about different plans and pricing, view webinars, access news releases, get the scoop on upcoming events, access documentation and other support, and get in touch with them — they'd love to hear from you!

Chapter **1**

Getting Up to Speed on Cloud Data Warehousing

I n one form or another, cloud computing and software-as-a-service (SaaS) have been around for decades. But cloud data warehouse-as-a-service (DWaaS) has only recently emerged as an alternative to conventional, on-premises data warehousing and similar solutions. Why now? What's changed? In this chapter, we answer these questions, and more.

We begin by defining what a data warehouse is and explore the evolution of data warehousing to show how this technology made its way to the cloud. Then we look at how organizations can benefit from cloud DWaaS and explain why more companies rely on cloud data warehousing to compete in today's data-driven economy.

Defining the Data Warehouse

A *data warehouse* is a computer system dedicated to storing and analyzing data to reveal trends, patterns, and correlations that provide information and insight. Traditionally, organizations have used data warehouses to store and integrate data collected from their internal sources (usually transactional databases), including marketing, sales, production, and finance. The data warehouse emerged when companies realized that analyzing data directly from those transactional databases slowed (and even crashed) them under the strain of their normal transaction activity and the workloads necessary to analyze that data. Hence, all that data was duplicated in a data warehouse for analysis, leaving the database to focus on transactions.

Over the years, data sources expanded beyond internal business operations and external transactions. They now include exponentially greater volumes, variety, and velocity of data from websites, mobile phones and apps, online games, online banking apps, and even machines. Most recently, organizations are capturing huge amounts of data from Internet of Things (IoT) devices.

The Evolution of Data Warehousing

Historically, businesses collected data in well-defined, highly structured forms at a reasonably predictable rate and volume. Even as the speed of older technologies advanced, data access and usage were carefully controlled and limited to ensure acceptable performance for every user, thanks to the scarcity of on-premises computing power and storage and the difficulty of increasing those resources. This required organizations to tolerate very long analytics cycles.

Times have changed (see Figure 1-1). Advances in technology mean organizations can make significant business decisions backed by large amounts of data.

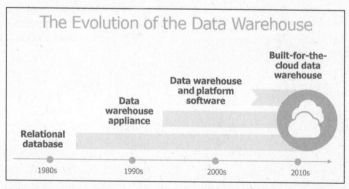

FIGURE 1-1: Traditional systems caused the cloud data warehouse to emerge.

It isn't just market leaders or mature companies. Smaller, nimble market entrants continue to transform well-established industries within months or just a couple of years. They're doing so with data to reveal opportunities and develop products and services that change how retail and business vendors engage their customers.

Recognizing the limitations of conventional data warehousing

Conventional data warehouses weren't designed to handle the volume, variety, and velocity of today's data. Newer systems designed to address these shortcomings struggle to accommodate the data access and analysis organizations now require. Today's challenges reveal:

>> Data sources are more numerous and varied, resulting in more-diverse data structures that must coexist in a single location to enable exhaustive and affordable analysis.

>> Traditional architectures inherently cause competition between users and data integration activities, making it difficult to simultaneously load new data into the data warehouse and provide users with adequate performance.

>> Loading data in batches at specific intervals is still common, but many organizations require continuous data loading (*microbatching*) and streaming data (*instant loading*).

>> Scaling up a conventional data warehouse to meet today's increasing storage and workload demands, when possible, is expensive, painful, and slow.

>> The more recent, alternative data platforms are often complex, requiring specialized skills and lots of tuning and configuration. This worsens with the growing number and diversity of data sources, users, and queries.

Technology and design to the rescue

The good news is that technology and data warehousing *architecture* (the design and building blocks of the modern data warehouse) have evolved to address the demands of the data–driven economy with the following innovations:

>> **The cloud:** A key factor driving the evolution of the modern data warehouse is the cloud. This creates access to near-infinite, low-cost storage; improved scalability; the outsourcing of data warehousing management and security to the cloud vendor; and the potential to pay for only the storage and computing resources actually used.

>> **Massively parallel processing (MPP):** MPP, which involves dividing a single computing operation to execute simultaneously across a large number of separate computer processors, emerged in the early 2000s. This division of labor facilitates faster storage and analysis of data when software is built to capitalize on the approach.

>> **Columnar storage:** Traditionally, databases stored records in rows, similar to how a spreadsheet appears. For example, this could include all information about a customer or a retail transaction. Retrieving data the traditional way required the system to read the entire row to get one element. This is laborious and time-consuming. With columnar storage, each data element of a record is stored in a column. With this approach, a user can query just one data element, such as gym members who have paid their dues, without having to read everything else in that entire record, which may include each member's ID number, name, age, address, city, state, payment information, and so on. This approach can provide a much faster response to these kinds of analytic queries.

>> **Vectorized processing:** This form of data processing for *data analytics* (the science of examining data to draw conclusions) takes advantage of the recent and revolutionary computer chip designs. This approach delivers much faster performance versus older data warehouse solutions built decades ago for older, slower hardware technology.

>> **Solid state drives (SSDs):** Unlike hard disk drives (HDDs), SSDs store data on flash memory chips, which accelerates data storage, retrieval, and analysis. A solution that takes advantage of SSDs can deliver significantly better performance.

For more about advances in technology and other trends driving the evolution of data warehousing, see Chapter 2.

Introducing the cloud data warehouse

Cloud data warehousing is a cost-effective way for companies to take advantage of the latest technology and architecture without the huge upfront cost of purchasing, installing, and configuring the required hardware, software, and infrastructure. The various cloud data warehousing options are generally grouped into three categories:

» **Traditional data warehouse software deployed on cloud infrastructure:** This option is similar to a conventional, on-premises data warehouse because it reuses the original code base. You still need IT expertise to build and manage the data warehouse. Although you don't have to purchase and install the hardware and software, you might still have to do significant configuration and tuning and perform operations, such as regular backups.

» **Traditional data warehouse hosted and managed in the cloud by a third party as a managed service:** With this option, the third-party provider supplies the IT expertise, but you're still likely to experience many of the same limitations of a conventional data warehouse. The data warehouse is hosted on hardware installed in a data center managed by the vendor. This is similar to what the industry referred to as an *application service provider (ASP)*. The customers still must specify in advance how much disk space and compute resources (CPUs and memory) they expect to use.

» **A true SaaS data warehouse:** With this option, often referred to as *DWaaS,* the vendor delivers a complete cloud data warehouse solution that includes all hardware and software, and nearly eliminates all of the tasks related to establishing and managing the performance, governance, and security required with a data warehouse. Clients typically pay only for the storage and computing resources they use, when they use them. This option should also scale up and down on demand by adding unlimited amounts of computing power dedicated to each workload, while an unlimited number of workloads operate concurrently without impacting performance.

For a more detailed comparison of cloud data warehousing solutions, turn to Chapter 5.

Why You Need a Cloud Data Warehouse

Any organization depending on data to better serve its customers, streamline its operations, and lead its industry will benefit from a cloud data warehouse. Unlike massive, traditional data warehouses, the cloud means businesses big and small can size their data warehouse to meet their needs and their budget, and dynamically grow and contract their system as things change from day to day and year to year.

Here are a few areas where cutting-edge cloud data warehouse technology can significantly improve a company's operations:

>> **Customer experience:** Monitoring end-user behavior in real time can help organizations tailor products, services, and special offers to the needs of individual consumers. With customer sentiment analysis, companies better understand customers by analyzing massive amounts of social media postings, tweets, and other online activity.

>> **Quality assurance:** Organizations can also use streaming data to monitor for early warning signs of customer service issues or product shortcomings. They can take action in minutes or hours, instead of days or weeks, which was not possible when the only data source was call center complaint logs.

>> **Operational efficiency:** *Operational intelligence* (OI) consists of monitoring the business and analyzing events to identify where an organization can reduce costs, boost margins, streamline processes, and respond to market forces more rapidly. By relieving your organization of managing a data warehouse, you can focus on analyzing data.

>> **Innovation:** Instead of only checking the rear-view mirror to understand an industry's recent past, companies can use new sources of data and data analytics (predictive, prescriptive, machine learning) to spot and capitalize on trends, thereby disrupting their industry before an unknown or unforeseen competitor does so first.

REMEMBER

Nearly all of a company's data is stored in a multitude of disparate databases. The key questions to ask are: How accessible is that data? How much will it cost to extract, store, and analyze all of it? What will happen if you don't? This is where cloud data warehousing comes into play.

Chapter **2**
Learning Why the Modern Data Warehouse Emerged

Cloud data warehousing emerged from the convergence of three major trends — changes in data sources, volume, and variety; increased demand for data access and analytics; and technology improvements that significantly increased the efficiency of data storage, access, and analytics. In this chapter, we describe these trends in greater detail and reveal how a data warehouse can take advantage of the benefits of cloud to address them.

Looking at Trends in Data: Volume, Variety, and Velocity

When we talk about data in this book, we're talking petabytes. One petabyte is equal to 1 million gigabytes. That's equal to about 500 billion pages of standard, printed text or 58,333 high-definition movies, each approximately two hours in length. Data pours in from the daily operations of a business, from people using websites and software applications on their mobile devices, and from the daily activity of digital and mechanical devices.

In this section, we focus on changes in data, and data use, that have led to demand for cloud data warehousing.

Managing the data tsunami

In the not-so-distant past, businesses generally managed data that was entered manually into the system by human beings. They also may have had data from external sources, such as customers, clients, and partners. The amount of data was relatively small and predictable, and the data was stored, managed, and secured in a company's data center, now known as an *on-premises method*.

Today, the business world is experiencing a data tsunami, with data available from a variety of sources already mentioned in this book and other sources too numerous and varied to list. The volume and variety of this data can quickly overwhelm a conventional, on-premises data warehouse and often causes data processing and analysis to hang or even crash the system, due to an overload of users and the workloads they process at any given time.

Adapting to the exponential increase of data requires a fresh perspective (see Figure 2-1). The conversation must shift from how big an organization's data warehouse must be to whether it can scale cost-effectively, without friction, and on the order of magnitude necessary to handle massive volumes of data.

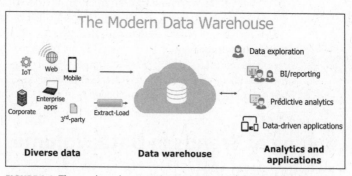

FIGURE 2-1: The modern data warehouse enables all data for all users.

REMEMBER

The use cases that cloud data warehousing has sparked continue to emerge. For example, SaaS-born companies and big enterprises that use the cloud to store their data are monetizing (selling) that data. They package it as a service and sell it to other organizations keen to make even better business decisions from the deepest possible insights.

Benefiting from data born in the cloud

Organizations have experienced a rapid adoption of SaaS, including customer relationship management (CRM) software, enterprise resource planning (ERP) software suites, advertising buying platforms, and online marketing tools, to name just a few. Thanks to the cloud, new SaaS companies can set up shop for the price of a laptop or two. These SaaS products create huge amounts of valuable data stored in the cloud. In addition, organizations realize SaaS vendors provide better security than what's possible in their own on-premises data centers.

Demand for SaaS/cloud applications has also grown. Ease of deployment pales to what on-premises applications require to get up and running. In the past, a company may have operated only five to ten significant enterprise applications that generated data. Now, it's normal for even midsize organizations to have hundreds or even thousands of applications, each with the potential of creating its own data silo — marketing data in one system, finance in another, product information in yet another — and none of them integrated for complete and optimal analysis.

With the majority of an organization's data now in the cloud, the natural place to integrate this data is also in the cloud. With cloud data warehousing, you're no longer forced to pull it inside your data center, which is expensive and time-consuming and makes less sense as the amount of cloud-native data grows.

Using machine-generated data

Machine-generated data is a key topic related to the *Internet of Things (IoT)* — an endless collection of devices that communicate data via the Internet, including smartphones, thermostats, refrigerators, oil rigs, home security systems, smart meters, and much more. Data collected and analyzed from IoT devices can enhance products and processes, monitor equipment, and predict needed maintenance to avoid failure.

But a lot of machine-generated data has a poor signal-to-noise ratio. It contains valuable data but also a lot of "noise." Therefore, you often must store all of it to find the valuable bits. In addition, a growing share of this data originates outside your data center. This makes cloud, and its near-infinite scalability, the natural location for storing and integrating this data.

Experimenting with data exploration

Analyzing data starts with data exploration — identifying interesting and valuable connections and serving them up to data users in the form of reports and analytics. Although data exploration isn't a new concept, the growth in data volume makes it a more resource-intensive exercise.

Data exploration often involves large data sets. It's also often experimental in nature, which complicates the ROI assessment needed to support the significant upfront cost of deploying a traditional, on-premises data warehouse. In response, the cloud can enable a data warehouse to scale up and down as needed and offers a pay-for-use model that lets organizations avoid the question of whether or not to make an expensive, upfront commitment.

Introducing data lakes

The growing need to have massive amounts of raw data in different formats, all in a single location, spawned what's now considered the legacy data lake. Organizations quickly realized that these solutions were cost prohibitive, since transforming that data and extracting valuable insight from it was nearly impossible.

But the original interest in data lakes made it clear that companies wanted to store all of their data in one location at a reasonable cost. By adding a modern cloud data warehouse to your existing data lake, or building your data lake within the data warehouse, you can easily achieve that original vision for the data lake: cost-effectively loading, transforming, and analyzing unlimited amounts of structured and semi-structured data — with near-unlimited storage and compute resources.

Exploring Trends in Reporting and Analytics

Data-driven decision-making is no longer relegated to the executive team or data scientists. It's now used to improve nearly every operational aspect of a company. But this increasing demand for data access and analytics across an organization can slow or crash a system as workloads compete for storage and compute resources from traditional data warehouses. Efficiency drops, which requires companies to invest more time and money in additional infrastructure to maintain the system.

In this section, we identify some of the trends changing how people access and use data and how those trends drive the need for modern, built-for-the-cloud data warehouse solutions.

Using elasticity to enable analytics

Here are a few scenarios where cloud-built elastic data warehousing can make it possible to do more with data:

>> Data exploration has many benefits. But no one really knows in advance the compute resources needed to analyze huge data sets, making on-demand, elastic scalability ideal for this kind of analysis.

>> Ad hoc data analysis, which emerges all the time, answers a single, specific, business question. Dynamic elasticity and dedicated resources for each workload enables these queries without slowing down other workloads.

>> Event-driven analytics demand constant data. They incorporate new data to update reports and dashboards on a continual basis, so senior managers can monitor the business in real time or near-real time. Ingesting and processing streaming data requires an elastic data warehouse to handle variations and spikes in data flow.

Replacing exhaustive preplanning with rapid iteration

Entrepreneurs typically have two paths to follow when ensuring the marketability of a new idea: exhaustive preplanning or rapid iteration. The first option is a traditional, time-consuming process that involves thinking through an opportunity or a new product idea, kicking ideas back and forth, and hoping it creates consumer demand. Rapid iteration involves quickly testing the idea in the market to iterate over and over until a viable version of the product shows success. From there, the process begins again.

Rapid iteration has emerged as the more effective process for dismantling established competitors and altering how an entire industry does business. But it requires high-speed collection and analysis of large amounts of accurate data to be successful. Advances in cloud data warehousing and analytics have made rapid iteration more practical, while preserving data accuracy.

CASE STUDY

MEETING INCREASED DEMAND FOR DATA ANALYTICS

Jana provides free, unrestricted Internet access to more than 30 million smartphone users in more than 15 emerging markets. With its mCent Android app, Jana shifts the cost of mobile Internet from customers to more than 4,000 brands via sponsored content.

When new, branded content or mCent features are introduced, Jana analyzes and measures key metrics, including user attention, lifetime user value, and key performance indicators (KPIs).

As Jana and its data grew, the company's initial analytics architecture could no longer efficiently serve its business. Queries slowed and table scans became unfeasible. Adding capacity and backup systems and administering Jana's open source data repository required more and more administration time.

As illustrated in the figure, Jana upgraded most of its data platform components to streamline its system with a cloud-built data warehouse to overcome these barriers and gain the following benefits:

- Keep pace with the business demands of processing and analyzing a rapidly growing stream of disparate data.

- Encourage an increased use of analytics throughout the company; 80 percent of Jana's employees access the data warehouse.

- Significantly reduce administration overhead.

Jana's transformation to a faster, cheaper, and more effective data warehouse.

Embedding analytics

For many companies, analytics operate as a separate and distinct business process. But a growing trend is to build analytics into business applications, which are increasingly built in the cloud. These applications handle significant variability in the number of users that query the applications and the number of queries (workloads) users run to analyze that data. The cloud facilitates data transfers from cloud-based applications to the organization's cloud data warehouse, where its scalability and elasticity can better support fluctuations in users and workloads.

Technology Musts for Any Modern Data Warehouse

Technology innovations can improve data warehousing and analytics with regard to availability, simplicity, cost, and performance. In this section, we focus on the key technologies that should be part of any modern data warehouse.

Cloud

The properties of the cloud make it particularly well-suited for data warehousing. We've mentioned these in other contexts, but it's important to know they came from the cloud:

>> **Unlimited resources:** Cloud infrastructure delivers near-unlimited resources, on demand, and within minutes or seconds. Organizations pay by the second only for what they use, making it possible to dynamically support any scale of users and workloads without compromising performance.

>> **Save money, focus on data:** Companies that choose a cloud-built solution avoid the costly, up-front investment of hardware, software, and other infrastructure, and the costs of maintaining, updating, and securing an on-premises system. They instead focus on analyzing data.

> **»** **Natural integration point:** By some estimates, as much as 80 percent of the data you want to analyze comes from applications outside your company's data center. Bringing that data together in the cloud is easier and cheaper than building an internal data center because you don't have to buy millions of dollars' worth of hardware and software up front and then pay technical staff to maintain those resources.

Columnar storage, processing

As mentioned earlier, columnar storage significantly improves the efficiency and performance of data storage, retrieval, and analysis, enabling quicker access to results for system users.

Solid state drives (SSDs)

Unlike hard disk drives (HDDs), SSDs store data on flash memory chips, which accelerate data storage, retrieval, and analysis. These improvements augment the computing power of data warehouses architected to use SSDs effectively.

NoSQL

NoSQL, short for *not only structured query language (SQL)*, describes a technology that enables the storing and analyzing of newer forms of data, such as data generated from machines and from social media, to enrich and expand an organization's data analytics. Traditional data warehouses don't accommodate these data types very well. Therefore, newer approaches, such as JSON, Avro, and XML, have emerged in recent years to handle these "semi-structured" data forms.

Some of these NoSQL systems were designed with the intent to replace traditional data warehouses but ended up complementing them only. To get value from semi-structured data, organizations often have to extract and transform data from a NoSQL system and load it into a traditional data warehouse for easy access by business users. As a result, this adds another layer of complexity and cost for companies (such as Jana; see the earlier case study) that attempt to capitalize on the benefits of both types of systems.

Therefore, the modern cloud-built data warehouse must incorporate, and optimize for, the ingestion and query of structured (traditional) and semi-structured data formats so organizations avoid paying for and managing two systems.

Chapter **3**

The Criteria for Selecting a Modern Data Warehouse

The trends discussed in Chapter 2 have led to a need and an opportunity for a new kind of data warehouse — one built for the volume, variety, and velocity of today's data, and for the new ways organizations use their data. Such a solution must take advantage of key technology innovations, including the cloud.

When you're in the market for a data warehouse, a checklist of criteria will help determine which alternative best meets your needs. Consider this chapter your checklist for finding the best data warehouse solution for your organization.

Meets Current and Future Needs

True elasticity has its business benefits, but there's more to that story. You should be able to scale both compute resources and storage independently, so you are not forced to add more storage when you really just need more compute, and vice versa. These are key capabilities of an elastic data warehouse.

Stores and Integrates All Data in One Place

Nontraditional, or semi-structured data, as discussed in previous chapters, can enrich the insight of data analytics beyond the limits of traditional data. But this requires a new approach to loading and transforming these new data types before an organization can analyze that data. Most traditional data warehouses sacrifice performance or flexibility to handle these data types. A modern data warehouse should eliminate the need to design and model rigid, traditional structures up front that would require transforming semi-structured data before loading. It should also optimize query performance against these data types while still in their native forms. Overall, the data warehouse should support diverse data with flexibility and avoid performance issues.

Efficiently loading all of your data into one location is crucial. But integrating all of those diverse data types for more-precise analytics is something else. A modern data warehouse should automatically integrate your semi-structured data, once confined to NoSQL systems, with structured data inherent to a traditional, corporate relational database. There should be nothing to install and configure, and tuning and performance should be built in. Most importantly, you shouldn't have to maintain and pay for two separate systems to manage all of your data.

Supports Existing Skills, Tools, and Expertise

Traditional data warehouses are outdated only because the technology spans four decades and is not easily re-engineered for the cloud. That also means the language they rely on, SQL, remains an industry mainstay. Because of this, there exists a broad array of mature and emerging data management, data transformation, integration, visualization, business intelligence, and analytics tools that communicate with a SQL data warehouse. The well-established role of standard SQL also means a huge number of people have SQL skills.

Traditional data warehouses support SQL but don't support the capabilities needed to effectively store and process semi-structured data. Many organizations have therefore turned to alternative approaches, such as NoSQL solutions. The limitations of these systems pose another problem. They require specialized knowledge and skills that aren't broadly available and might not support SQL. A modern data warehouse should be architected with leading technology but built on inclusive and established standards (such as SQL), and should be compatible with other skills and tools commonly available in the industry, such as Spark, Python, and R computing languages.

Saves Your Organization Money

A conventional data warehouse can cost millions of dollars in licensing fees, hardware, and services; the time and expertise required to set up, manage, deploy, and tune the warehouse; and the costs to secure and back up data. In addition, building a data warehouse that meets the business requirements and takes full advantage of the volume and variety of today's data is often cost prohibitive for any organization.

A modern data warehouse should meet these challenges at a much lower price point. For example, does it scale storage and compute separately so you pay only for the resources you need? Does it also scale workloads and concurrency? Will it support diverse data structures and integrate diverse data in one place? Will it experience minimal to no downtime and provide the choice of delivering upgrades automatically or in a staged format? And finally, can it do all of this automatically without the complexity, expense, and headache of manually tweaking and tuning the system to get the best performance? (See Chapter 5 for comparing cloud data warehouses.)

REMEMBER

With cloud data warehousing, your service fee should cover everything for a small fraction of the cost of a conventional, on-premises solution. But not all cloud-based solutions are the same. Their differences also determine how much a customer must pay, in one way or another, to gain valuable data insight.

Provides Data Resiliency and Recovery

Many types of data warehouse failures can cause data loss or inconsistencies. Therefore, your data warehouse must keep your data safe, up to date, and available. Traditional data warehouses typically protect data by performing periodic backups, which consume valuable compute resources and interfere with ongoing workloads. Periodic backups also require additional storage and often fail to include the most recent data, resulting in data inconsistencies.

A modern data warehouse should manage itself when it comes to ensuring the durability, resiliency, and availability of the system. It shouldn't interfere with any ongoing workloads, degrade performance, or result in service unavailability due to backup processes running in the background. And it should be cheap, with clever ways to preserve your data without having to copy and move it somewhere else. Finally, having a multi-cloud architecture gives you portability to relocate data and workloads as your business expands, both among geographic regions and among major cloud vendors, such as Amazon, Microsoft, and Google.

Secures Data at Rest and in Transit

Data security covers the following two main areas:

>> **Confidentiality:** Preventing unauthorized access to data

>> **Integrity:** Ensuring the data isn't modified or corrupted, it's properly governed, and quality remains

A modern data warehouse must also support multilevel *role-based access control (RBAC)*. This ensures users have access only to the data they're permitted to see. For better security, require *multifactor authentication (MFA)*. With MFA, when a user logs in, the system sends a secondary verification request, often to a mobile phone. The passcode sent to the phone must then be entered. This ensures that an unauthorized person with a stolen username and password cannot access the system.

Data governance ensures a company's data is properly accessed and used, and that all data is managed and safeguarded to thwart breaches and to comply with detailed regulations. It also requires rigorous oversight to maintain the quality of the data your company shares with constituents. Bad data can lead to missed or poor business decisions, loss of revenue, and increased costs. Data stewards — charged with overseeing data quality — can identify when data is corrupt or inaccurate, when it's not being refreshed often enough to be relevant, or when it's being analyzed out of context.

Encrypting the data, which means applying an encryption algorithm to translate the clear text into cipher text, is another required security feature. A bigger part of the solution is "key management." Once you encrypt your data, you'll use an encryption key to decrypt it. In addition to protecting data, you have to protect the key that decodes the data. How long do you use the same key? What happens if the key is compromised? All of this must be managed. The data warehouse should use a hierarchical key-wrapping approach, which encrypts the encryption keys, as well as a robust key-rotation process, which limits the number of times any single key is used.

In addition, the solution provider of a modern cloud data warehouse must perform periodic security testing, known as *penetration testing*, to proactively check for vulnerabilities. The vendor must administer these measures consistently and automatically without impacting performance.

For a full discussion about cloud data warehouse security and governance, see Chapter 8.

Choose a data warehouse with industry-standard, end-to-end security. Find a solution that has passed security audits such as SOC 1/SOC 2 Type II and ISO/IEC 27001.

Streamlines the Data Pipeline

The *data pipeline* refers primarily to the *extract, transform, and load (ETL)* processes that import data into the warehouse and in a format that supports queries. A slow data pipeline forces users, such as analysts, to spend too much time waiting to access data. The rapid growth in the diversity, number, and size of nonrelational data streaming in from multiple sources compounds the problem.

A modern data warehouse should reduce the overall complexity of the process to move data through the data pipeline faster. Modern solutions should be able to efficiently load semi-structured data in its native format and make it immediately available for query without needing additional and intricate systems, such as NoSQL, to transform data. This allows users to immediately access data in the same way they query a SQL database. Such solutions can provide access to new data exponentially faster, reducing the ingestion and transformation process from a day to less than an hour.

Optimizes Your Time to Value

Deploying a solution should not be a major undertaking, and crucial aspects that were once manual should be automated. Most of all, the solution you choose should be available all the time to all users and encompass all data types at a fraction of the cost of traditional systems. Such a system should deliver immediate data insight to help streamline an organization and increase its ability to serve customers and lead its industry.

» Slashing storage and compute costs

» Taking advantage of dynamic elasticity

» Outsourcing administration and security

Chapter **4**
On-Premises versus Cloud Data Warehousing

When you're in the market for a new data warehouse, the first choice to consider is where you want your data warehouse located: your organization's data center or in the cloud and provided as software as a service (SaaS). Traditional on-premises data warehousing is a mature, well-established technology designed long before the cloud became a viable platform. With the rapid adoption of cloud, there's a need for data warehouse solutions that can take full advantage of what the cloud offers. In this chapter, we present the key considerations for cloud data warehousing as we compare it to traditional, on-premises systems.

Evaluating Time to Value

Deploying a conventional data warehouse (see Chapter 3) can take at least a year and extend to a multiyear project before you extract insight from your data. The agility of business today means key stakeholders who support the project, and key business and technical enablers responsible for the project's success, might leave the team or the company before the project goes live. Such a long cycle also exposes the project to economic downturns, company revenue shortfalls, and the risk of never implementing the project due to scope creep.

In addition, on-premises solutions aren't geared to handle today's semi-structured data. That requires adding an open source, NoSQL platform, which adds another layer of complexity and lengthens the implementation phase of a new data warehouse.

Done right, a cloud data warehouse can be up and running in weeks or just a few months. Therefore, most of the time required to get up and running should be spent extracting data from your other data sources and configuring a front-end analytics tool to extract insight from the data warehouse.

Accounting for Storage and Computing Costs

On-premises data warehouses are expensive in terms of hardware, software, and administration. Hardware costs can include the costs of servers, additional storage devices, data center space to house the hardware, a high-speed network to access the data, and the power and redundant power supplies needed to keep the system up and running. If your warehouse is mission critical, add the costs for configuring a disaster recovery site. Organizations also frequently pay hundreds of thousands of dollars in software licensing fees for data warehouse software and add-on packages. Additional end-users, including customers and suppliers who are given access to the data warehouse, can significantly increase those costs. Then add the ongoing cost for annual support contracts, which often comprise 20 percent of the original license cost. Additionally, an on-premises data warehouse needs specialized, *information technology (IT)* personnel to deploy and maintain the system. This creates a potential bottleneck when issues arise and keeps responsibility for the system with the customer, not the vendor.

A cloud data warehouse replaces the initial CapEx and ongoing cost of an on-premises system with simple OpEx usage-based pricing. You pay a monthly fee based on how much storage and computing resources you actually use. Conservatively speaking, the annualized cost for a cloud data warehouse solution can be one-tenth that of a similar, on-premises system.

Sizing, Balancing, and Tuning

For optimum performance, an on-premises data warehouse must be modeled, sized, balanced, and tuned, which requires a significant up-front investment along with ongoing monitoring and administration costs. Such a configuration often includes:

- » Number and speed of central processing units (CPUs)
- » Amount of memory
- » Number and size of disks for required storage capacity
- » Input/output (I/O) *bandwidth* (a measure of how much data can be transferred at a given time)
- » A custom data model defining the warehouse structure, included data types, and update frequency

With an on-premises data warehouse, organizations often size their system for peak usage, which may represent only a small period of the year. For example, a company may need the full power of the data warehouse only at the end of each financial quarter or year. But it must pay for that peak capacity 24 hours a day, every day, because the system can't easily scale up or down.

Elastic cloud data warehousing delivers two key advantages:

- » The complexities and cost of capacity planning and administration — sizing, balancing, and tuning the system — should be built into the system, automated, and covered by the cost of your subscription.

- » The same goes for dynamically provisioning storage and compute resources on the fly to meet the demands of your changing workloads in peak and steady usage periods. Capacity is having whatever you need whenever you need it. But not all workloads are created equal. An elastic cloud data warehouse lets you get very granular regarding what resources are allocated to which users and workloads.

Considering Data Preparation and ETL Costs

An on-premises data warehouse must extract data from all of your data sources. Then it must transform that data to adhere to the often rigid data structure inside the system *before* loading it into the warehouse. A key challenge includes adhering to a finite and expensive amount of processing capacity and storage. As a result, data transformation must happen outside normal business hours to avoid competing with other data processing jobs. This is expensive. In addition, semi-structured data doesn't arrive in consistent rows and columns inherent to traditional data structures. The data is also high-volume, high-velocity data.

The best cloud-built solutions can load semi-structured data directly without transforming it. These solutions can provide access to fresh data up to 50 times faster than a traditional data warehouse. In addition, the lower cost of unlimited cloud storage provides data analysts access to all of the data instead of limiting them to periodic aggregates of that data.

CASE STUDY

OPTIMIZING A DATA PIPELINE

DoubleDown, an online gaming studio, added a NoSQL system to its data pipeline to prepare data for loading into its data warehouse. But this approach meant DoubleDown's daily event log (user clicks and other data generated by gamers' activities) required long processing times. The company couldn't access one day's data until 3 p.m. the next day. Even worse, if one of its data computing clusters went down, the company lost data.

DoubleDown chose a system that could directly load its semi-structured data without transforming it first, making that data immediately available for queries. This improved the quality and performance of its data pipeline by getting data to analysts nearly 100 times faster — in 15 minutes versus 24 hours, eliminating nearly all of the frequent failures in the company's previous pipeline, providing analysts full data granularity instead of periodic aggregates, and reducing the cost of DoubleDown's data pipeline by 80 percent.

DoubleDown analysts now have immediate access to data from new product releases for faster, data-driven decisions.

Adding the Cost of Specialized Business Analytics Tools

As mentioned in Chapter 3, traditional, on-premises data warehouses aren't geared to handle the volume, variety, and velocity of today's data. As a result, organizations operate two data platforms: an on-premises, enterprise SQL data warehouse for storage of traditional relational data, and a NoSQL big data platform, which can run on-premises or in the cloud, for storing nonrelational data.

Unfortunately, these newer systems bring a lot of complexity to manage and require specialized tools and expertise that aren't nearly as prevalent as SQL tools and expertise. After all, SQL has been around for decades, while NoSQL systems are relative newcomers.

The ideal cloud data warehousing solution delivers the best of both worlds — the flexibility to integrate relational and nonrelational data along with support for the readily available SQL tools and skills for querying that data.

TIP

When you're in the market for a new data warehouse, consider the cost and availability of the skills and expertise required to manage the data warehouse as well as the many analytics and other tools used in conjunction with a data warehouse.

Making Allowances for Scaling and Elasticity

Conventional data warehouses are prone to system slowdowns and crashes as users and processes compete for limited resources. These systems tightly connect storage and compute onto a single computer *cluster* (a group of computers), making it costly to increase one without increasing the other.

Newer, cloud-built data warehouse solutions provide virtually unlimited storage and compute; however, consider a data warehouse that scales storage separate from compute (see Figure 4-1). Ideally, the cloud data warehouse should scale in three ways:

>> **Storage:** Cloud storage is inherently scalable, easily adjusting the amount of storage to meet changing needs.

>> **Compute:** The resources used for processing data loads and queries should easily scale up or down, at any time, as the number and intensity of the workloads change.

>> **Users and workloads (concurrency):** Solutions with fixed computing resources slow as users and workloads increase. Organizations are often forced to replicate data into separate data marts, shift some workloads outside of normal business hours, and queue users to preserve performance. Only the cloud can enable a data warehouse to "scale out" by adding dedicated compute clusters of any size to a near-infinite number of users or workloads that all access a single copy of the data but without impacting each other's performance.

Look for a cloud solution that decouples storage from compute, so both can scale easily and independently of each other to keep costs low. The solution should also scale out, or horizontally, to support more users and workloads without harming performance.

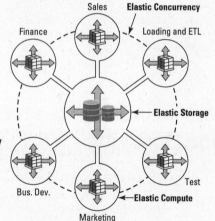

FIGURE 4-1: The ideal data warehouse should scale in three ways.

Decreasing Delays and Downtime

Many companies with on-premises solutions have two main complaints. They must wait hours or more than a day before data collected the previous day is in the warehouse and available. They must wait the same time for a complex query to run on a large data set. In some cases, multiple concurrent processes can freeze or crash the system, extending delays and downtime.

With virtually unlimited storage and compute resources, cloud data warehouse solutions, architected as dynamically elastic, are better equipped to scale up, down, and out to meet increased demands. However, decreasing delays and eliminating unplanned downtime requires more than simply ramping up system resources. Better solutions streamline the data pipeline and store data to make queries run more efficiently without manual tuning.

Look for solutions that address all these types of performance issues and that will minimize downtime. How quickly you can access your data and analytics can significantly affect your operations and your ability to maintain a competitive edge.

Considering the Costs of Security Issues

A single breach can quickly turn into a public relations nightmare and result in lost business and steep fines from regulatory agencies. Although the cloud attracts the fear of security risks, it can be more secure than your data center.

If you opt for an on-premises data warehouse, you're solely responsible for securing sensitive data, which involves careful and constant attention to firewall protection; security protocols; data encryption, at rest and in transit; user roles and privileges; and monitoring and adapting to emerging security threats.

Effective data security is complex and costly to implement, especially in terms of human resources. Poorly implemented security measures expose you to even more costs if breached.

Because cloud data warehousing providers serve a number of customers, they can afford the expertise and resources to provide industrial-strength, end-to-end data warehouse security. Look for a provider that ensures industry-standard, end-to-end encryption to secure data both at rest and in transit.

Paying for Data Protection and Recovery

On-premises data warehouses are vulnerable to data loss from equipment failure, power outages or surges, theft or vandalism, and disasters (fire, flood, earthquake, and so on). To protect your data, you must back it up regularly and store backups at a remote location. A backup power supply is also necessary to prevent data loss and ensure your data warehouse is always available to process incoming data and queries. If disaster does strike, you'll need skilled personnel in place to recover data, using the most recent backups. If your data warehouse is mission critical, you may also need a geographically separated disaster recovery site (an additional data center) along with the software, licenses, and processes to ensure automatic failover so there's no gap in service.

The cloud provides an ideal solution for data protection and recovery. By its nature, it stores data off premises. Some cloud-based solutions automatically back up data to two or more separate physical locations. If the data centers are geographically isolated, they also provide built-in disaster recovery. Cloud data centers have redundant power supplies, so they remain up and running even during lengthy power outages. Cloud providers can deliver these protections at a much lower cost than you can, by distributing the cost over thousands of clients.

TIP

If you do not want to administer your own data backups, be sure to ask your potential cloud data warehouse provider how it configures its service. Likewise, if you need disaster recovery protection, confirm the provider's architecture uses geographically separated centers. Also ask if your provider offers its solution across multiple cloud providers in case a disaster requires you to switch to an instance of your data warehouse in another cloud.

Chapter **5**

Comparing Cloud Data Warehouse Solutions

The growing adoption of cloud has caused legacy on–premises vendors and recent market entrants to offer cloud versions of their data warehouse products. Of course, no two solutions are the same. In this chapter, we explain some of the differences and what to look for among cloud data warehouses.

Understanding Approaches to Data Warehousing in the Cloud

The following cloud approaches offer significantly different data warehouse capabilities:

» **Infrastructure-as-a-service (IaaS):** Requires the customer to install traditional data warehouse software on computers provided by the cloud platform provider. The customer manages all aspects of the cloud hardware and data warehouse software. The capabilities of the data warehouse are identical to the same software deployed using on-premises hardware.

» **Platform-as-a-service (PaaS):** With this hybrid approach, the data warehouse vendor provides the hardware and software as a cloud service, and the vendor manages the hardware deployment, software installation, and software configuration. The customer manages, tunes, and optimizes the software.

>> **Software-as-a-service (SaaS):** The data warehouse vendor provides all hardware and software, including all aspects of managing the hardware and software. Typically included in the service: software and hardware upgrades, security, availability, data protection, and optimization.

In all of these scenarios, the task of purchasing, deploying, and configuring the data center space, and the hardware to support the data warehouse, transfers from the customer to the vendor. Beyond that advantage, the benefits and drawbacks of the different offerings vary from ease of use to security and availability.

REMEMBER

If a data warehouse provider merely supplies access to its traditional data warehouse via the cloud, the solution is likely to resemble its original, on-premises architecture and functionality.

Comparing Architectures

Many vendors offer a cloud data warehouse originally designed and deployed for on-premises environments. These traditional architectures were created long before the cloud and its benefits emerged as a viable option. Alternatively, any data warehouse solution built for the cloud should capitalize on the benefits of the cloud (see Figure 5-1). To identify a solution built on a cloud-optimized architecture, look for the following characteristics:

>> Centralized storage for all data

>> Independent scaling of compute and storage resources

>> Near-unlimited concurrency without competing for resources

>> Load and query data simultaneously without degrading performance

>> Replicate data across multiple regions and clouds to enhance business continuity and simplify expansion

>> Share data without setting up APIs or establishing cumbersome ETL procedures

>> A robust metadata service that applies across the entire system. (*Metadata* is data about other data, such as file size, author, and when it was created.) A cloud-optimized architecture also takes advantage of storage-as-a-service, where data storage expands and contracts automatically and transparently to the user. Data storage designed for older architectures is expensive and has limited scalability.

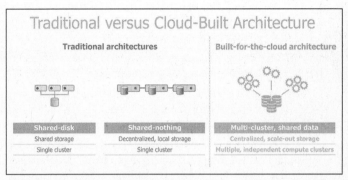

FIGURE 5-1: How a cloud-optimized architecture streamlines performance.

Assessing Data Diversity Management

A key factor driving the adoption of cloud data warehousing stems from the growing volume of data that originates in the cloud — outside a company's data center. In most cases, this nonrelational data must be transformed before being loaded into a traditional data warehouse on premises or in the cloud. This approach adds significant complexity and delays to accessing new data.

With this greater volume and variety of data, the cloud has become a natural integration point. An ideal way to address this issue is with a cloud data warehouse that can handle both relational and nonrelational data, and without having to transform the nonrelational data or compromise performance during the data loading or query processing.

REMEMBER

Data must be transformed before it's loaded into a traditional, cloud-based warehouse. Alternatively, the organization must buy and maintain an additional system to handle nonrelational data.

Gauging Scale and Elasticity

Not all cloud data warehouses feature the same type of elasticity. Advanced solutions can scale up and down, on the fly, and without taking the system offline or putting it into a read–only mode.

TIP

Consider the drawbacks of solutions that don't scale well:

>> A cloud data warehouse that requires manual reconfiguration involves careful planning and coordination with the vendor to scale resources.

>> Scaling may require downtime or a switch to read-only mode to redistribute data and reconfigure the system.

>> Most cloud data warehouse offerings bundle compute and storage on the same node, requiring customers to scale both when they need to increase just one or the other.

>> Most are "cloud-washed" versions of on-premises solutions, so you'll have to buy an oversized but underutilized configuration for when you need peak usage. Eventually, you'll exceed the resources available and face costly upgrades.

Comparing Concurrency Capabilities

Concurrency is the ability to perform two or more tasks simultaneously or to allow two or more users access to a computing solution. In a traditional data warehouse, fixed compute and storage resources limit concurrency. With cloud, however, compute and storage are not fixed. Cloud–optimized architectures support concurrency in the following two ways:

>> Multiple users can query the same data simultaneously without degrading performance.

>> Loading and querying can happen concurrently, enabling multiple, simultaneous workloads without resource contention.

Ensuring Support for SQL and Other Tools

Almost all business intelligence (BI); extract, transform, and load (ETL); and data analytics tools can communicate with a data warehouse that supports standard SQL. However, not all cloud data warehousing solutions fully support standard SQL. For example, big data solutions positioned as "cloud data warehouses" are often NoSQL solutions and have only incomplete or nonstandard SQL support. Although supporting these newer analytic tools is important, SQL remains the industry standard for querying data. Your data warehouse should support SQL tools for data management, data transformation, data integration, visualization, BI, and other types of analytics.

Checking Backup/Recovery Support

With on-premises and many cloud data warehousing solutions, customers must protect their own data with backup and data replication tools. However, some cloud data warehouse solutions include data protection as part of the service.

REMEMBER

For optimum protection, look for a solution that automatically saves past versions of data or automatically duplicates data for use as an online backup. The solution should also allow for self-service recovery of lost or corrupted data by way of replication across regions within the same cloud provider or across multiple cloud providers for complete business continuity.

Confirming Resiliency and Availability

Resiliency is the ability of the data warehouse to continue to function automatically in the midst of component, network, or even data center failure. *Availability* is the ability users have to access the system at all times (known as "uptime"). Cloud data warehouse services vary as to how much the customer is responsible for availability and resiliency. At the most basic level, a cloud data warehouse service may require the customer to handle system monitoring to detect and possibly prevent a failure. The customer may also have to administer data replication, so a duplicate copy of the data warehouse is available in case of a failure. At the other end of the spectrum, the vendor provides monitoring, replication, and automatic failover as part of the service.

Availability is also a factor for software upgrades. Different vendors take different approaches during the upgrade:

>> **Basic:** Customers manage upgrades and related downtime.

>> **Better:** The vendor manages upgrades and informs users of upcoming upgrades, so they can plan for the downtime.

>> **Best:** The vendor provides transparent upgrades without involving users or subjecting them to any downtime. The vendor also allows customers to opt in or out of automatic upgrades, so they can receive them when they desire.

Look for how many "9s" of availability the cloud data warehouse solution supports (99.9XX percent uptime).

TIP

Optimizing Performance

One of the great promises of the cloud is the ability to have huge amounts of resources available that you can pay for only when you need them. Look for a cloud data warehouse solution that can optimize performance on demand and that eliminates administrative effort to incorporate new resources.

Steer clear of data warehouses that disrupt or delay activity to add or subtract resources. Some solutions also require administrative work, including redistributing data and recalculating metadata.

REMEMBER

Evaluating Cloud Data Security

The cloud is often perceived as less secure than on-premises data storage, yet cloud solutions have gained increasing acceptance due to break-ins into "secure," on-premises data centers. These incidents reveal that companies are limited in their ability to secure their own data. Cloud data warehousing offerings shift responsibility for physical data center security to the solution vendor, but beware: Security features vary among vendors:

>> Basic cloud data warehouse offerings provide only some security capabilities, leaving things such as encryption, access control, and security monitoring to the customer.

>> Other solutions offer features such as encryption and access controls, which customers can choose to turn on, but they leave the system vulnerable if not enabled.

>> Cloud data warehouse offerings that are more service-oriented incorporate features for security and provide encryption, encryption key management, key rotation, intrusion detection, and more, as part of the service.

Accounting for Administration

Traditional data warehouses require a significant amount of the customer's time, effort, and expertise. One or more database administrators (DBAs) must perform software patches and upgrades, data partitioning and repartitioning, index management, workload management, statistics updates, security management and monitoring, backups and replication, query tuning and rewriting, and more.

At a base level, a cloud data warehouse solution that's built on older, on-premises technology still requires the customer to manage all of these aspects. Newer data warehousing offerings reduce or eliminate much of this management overhead through new designs and automation.

Enabling Secure Data Sharing

Many businesses can enhance their operations by tapping into third-party data repositories, services, and streams. Traditional data-sharing methods, such as FTP, APIs, and email, require you to copy data and send it to consumers. These cumbersome, costly, and risky methods are based on sharing static data, which quickly becomes dated and must be continually refreshed with more-current versions. Chapter 6 details how a cloud-built data warehouse enables live, governed, and secure data sharing.

TIP

Today's robust data-sharing methods allow you to exchange live data without moving it from place to place.

Allowing Global Data Replication

Data replication creates multiple copies of your data in the cloud. Having this type of global footprint is not only essential for disaster recovery and business continuity: It also comes in handy if you want to share data with a global customer base without setting up ETL pipelines among regions. Top data warehouse vendors allow you to easily share data among geographic regions and across multiple clouds, including Amazon Web Services (AWS), Microsoft Azure, and Google Cloud Platform (GCP). These global replication capabilities broaden your markets, make it easier to engage partners, and enable a more complete ecosystem for analytics and data sharing.

Ensuring Workload Isolation

A key factor in the speed and performance of a data warehouse is its ability to isolate workloads. To be effective, the cloud data warehouse should easily configure multiple pools of compute resources (of varying sizes) to separate the workloads of users and processes that need to run concurrently. This eliminates contention and provides resources sized to each workload. Ideally, these separate workloads should access the same data simultaneously and turn on and off easily, based on need.

Enabling All Use Cases

In traditional environments, different data systems handle different use cases — a data warehouse for operational reporting, data marts for departmental reporting and analytics, data lakes for data exploration, and specialized tools for activities such as predictive analytics. Each of these requires hardware, a copy of data, individual management, and so on.

To bring these diverse use cases together in the cloud, a data warehouse should support fast and efficient ways to clone multiple copies of tables, schema, and databases but without incurring the headache and cost of storage involved with traditional forms of duplicating data. A cloud data warehouse should also make it easy to recover from errors or problems created by data transformation jobs with features such as time travel, which enables simple access and rollback to previous versions of data.

Chapter **6**

Enabling Data Sharing

Data sharing is the act of providing access to data — both within an enterprise and between enterprises that have determined they have valuable assets to share. The organization that makes its data available, or shares its data, is a *data provider*. The organization that wants to use the shared data is a *data consumer*. Any organization can be a data provider, a data consumer, or both.

In addition to all the data organizations generate and share internally, many enhance their operations by tapping into third-party data repositories, services, and streams. For example, a financial services organization might tap into various market, financial, and economic indicators to create better data models, which in turn help it create new product offerings for its customers.

There's an abundance of potential value to unlock from the world's burgeoning data sources, internally and through external marketplaces and exchanges. Until recently, however, no technology existed for sharing data without a significant amount of risk, cost, headache, and delay. Although the commercial use of data sharing has been around for nearly a century, all methods to date have been limiting. Imagine the possibilities if all organizations could have on-demand access to ready-to-use, live data and could make immediate use of it. Data would no longer have to be deconstructed by the data provider, moved to the data consumer, and reconstructed by the data consumer. It would be instantly accessible and ready to use inside a secure, governed environment.

Confronting Technical Challenges

Traditional data sharing methods, such as File Transfer Protocol (FTP), cloud storage (Amazon S3, Box, Dropbox, and others), application programming interfaces (APIs), and email, require you to make a copy of the shared data and send it to your data consumers. These cumbersome, costly, and risky methods produce static data, which quickly becomes dated and must be refreshed with more current versions, requiring constant data movement and management.

New data sharing technologies enable organizations to easily share slices of their data, and receive shared data, in a secure and governed way. They don't require data movement; extract, transform, load (ETL) technology; or constant updates to keep data current. There's no need to transfer data via FTP or to configure APIs to link applications. Because data is shared rather than copied, no additional cloud storage is required. With this new architecture, data providers can easily and securely publish data for instant discovery, query, and enrichment by data consumers, as shown in Figure 6-1.

Efficient Data-Sharing Architecture

FIGURE 6-1: An efficient architecture for real-time data sharing.

A multitenant cloud-built data warehouse supplies the ideal platform for a data sharing service because it enables authorized members of a cloud ecosystem to tap into live, read-only versions of the data. Data providers can share data with vendors, supply chain partners, logistics partners, customers, and many other constituents. These cloud-built solutions leverage the latest advancements in cloud computing and data warehousing. Rather than physically transferring data to internal or external consumers, the warehouse enables read-only access to a governed portion of the live data set via SQL.

Achieving Data Sharing Success

Most organizations that embark on a data sharing journey follow a familiar progression:

1. **Internal collaboration:** Data is shared within the company among its business units and subsidiaries, improving collaboration and breaking down data silos.

2. **Business insights:** Having more-complete data improves collaboration and drives better business insights as data sharing becomes the norm.

3. **Customer analytics:** The company builds customer-facing analytics to improve the value of a product or service — the first step toward data monetization.

4. **Advanced analytics:** As customers request more data, the company develops custom analytics services to provide customers with rich information from its data.

5. **Data services:** The company leverages internal data sets to also provide customers with data augmentation services, such as data modeling, data enrichment, and data analytics.

6. **Data exchange:** The company looks for ways to improve its data products by sourcing external data and offering its data products to a wider audience, typically via a data marketplace or data exchange.

Monetizing Your Data

Most organizations already share data or plan to do so, but they might overlook how to monetize their data. There's an immense and rapidly expanding marketplace for monetizing data. In IDC's "2019 Predictions for Digital Transformation," the research firm predicted that 80 percent of enterprises will create data management and monetization capabilities by 2020, and that by 2023, 95 percent of entities will have incorporated new digital key performance indicator (KPI) sets.

TIP

With the right data sharing architecture, you can easily analyze more of your data to discover new products, services, and market opportunities.

MAXIMIZING REVENUE OPPORTUNITIES

CASE STUDY

Environics Analytics is one of North America's leading data analytics companies. To deliver data-driven insights to more than 3,000 clients, Environics ingests and analyzes large amounts of demographic, location, and consumer data.

Environics recently moved these analytic activities into a cloud-built data warehouse that can handle any amount of data and any number of workloads. An embedded data exchange service enables customers to discover and instantly obtain new data. According to Sean Howard, senior vice president of product development at Environics, having a secure data sharing service offers a convenient data-delivery mechanism and presents immense opportunities for growing revenue. The cloud platform quickly scales up or down to meet each user's analytic needs — without help from the IT team.

Previously, data scientists at Environics stored data sets on their computers and shared finished products with clients via FTP, which created internal confusion and inhibited growth. Exploring massive data sets containing billions of rows of events required constant support from the IT team to install hardware, build SQL server environments, optimize query performance, and monitor the usage of storage and compute resources.

Now, having an analytic environment that scales on demand allows data scientists to confidently prototype large data sets from any industry, source, or file type. They can convert billions of raw data points into viable data products. The secure data sharing service boosts customer loyalty, reduces fulfillment costs, and eliminates unnecessary file transfers — while dramatically simplifying version management.

Retailers, banks, credit unions, real estate firms, nonprofits, and government agencies use the data exchange to help them make informed decisions about consumers and markets. Environics is now experimenting with Internet of Things (IoT) data and other big data sources, thanks to a continuous data ingestion service that expedites data loading and enables near real-time analytics. "Participation in the data exchange will drive real business growth and help us get our data in front of more potential clients," Howard said.

Chapter 7

Maximizing Options with a Multi-Cloud Strategy

Having a data warehouse that can span multiple regions and multiple clouds offers tremendous advantages for data sharing, business continuity, and geographic penetration. According to the "2019 State of the Cloud" Report by Flexera, 84 percent of organizations have a multi-cloud strategy, reflecting the realities of the market. Whether it's Amazon Web Services, Microsoft Azure, or Google Cloud Platform, each cloud service addresses slightly different needs.

For organizations that want global reach with their data warehouse, a cross-cloud strategy makes sense: It enables the free and secure movement of data anywhere in the world while also allowing you to select cloud storage vendors that best meet your needs. For example, each of the departments within your organization might have unique cloud requirements. Rather than demand all business units use the same provider, a multi-cloud strategy allows each unit to use the cloud that works best for that unit. If this flexibility is important to you, look for a provider that supports multiple cloud environments and offers cross-cloud support.

Understanding Cross-Cloud

Multi-cloud means you can store your data in several different clouds. *Cross-cloud* means you can access data from all of those clouds simultaneously, seamlessly migrate analytic operations from one cloud to another, and share data among clouds. This is the holy grail of cloud data warehousing because you aren't tied to one cloud vendor. Why is this so important?

>> It's a strategic advantage for global companies because not all cloud providers operate in all regions.

>> It's useful if you acquire a company that has standardized on a cloud different from the one you're using.

>> If you plan to share or monetize your data, you'll expand your addressable market if you have a unified data management platform that spans regions and clouds.

In the following sections, we review the technologies that make a cross-cloud data warehouse possible.

TIP

Work with a data warehouse vendor that's done the hard work to resolve the differences among cloud configurations and built its solution on a common code base that spans all clouds.

Leveraging Global Replication

Data replication is the process of storing data in more than one location to ensure data availability during a regional outage. It's also the fundamental technology that allows you to share data across regions and clouds. Data warehouses need advanced data replication technology to maximize regional deployment options, enable business continuity, and expand operations worldwide.

Your data warehouse platform should make cross-region and cross-cloud replication possible, without reducing the performance of operations against your primary data.

Minimizing service disruption

Cross-cloud data warehouse replication is important for business-critical disaster recovery scenarios. In the event of an outage, it ensures you can instantly resume data processing activities without incurring any downtime (see Figure 7-1). However, without the right data replication technology, restoring geo-backups for large data warehouses can take hours or days. Will that meet your recovery time objectives?

Ask your data warehouse vendor if it supports instant access and recovery for databases of any size, in any cloud, and in any region. If a disaster occurs in a particular part of the world, you should be able to immediately access data replicated in a different region or cloud service. Find out if your data warehouse provider replicates databases and keeps them synchronized across cloud platforms and regions.

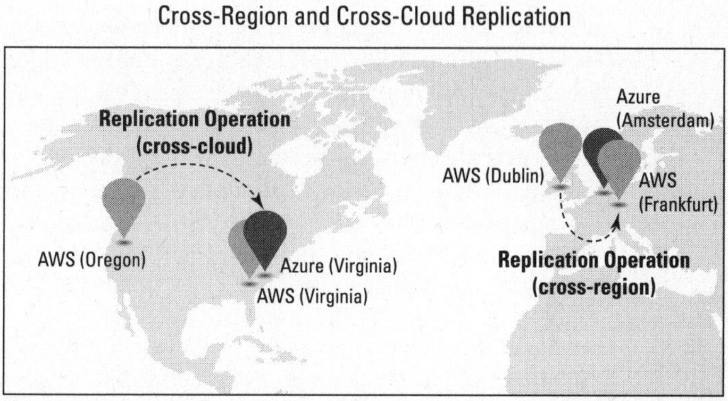

Cross-Region and Cross-Cloud Replication

FIGURE 7-1: Global data replication ensures business continuity during outages.

Supporting multiple clouds

Data portability is a widespread challenge for all organizations that have large amounts of data. Each public cloud provider has different levels of regional penetration. Moving data and workloads among geographic regions and clouds is easier with a cross-cloud architecture.

Data portability simplifies regulatory compliance if your industry requires your data remain within a certain country or region. Merging with or acquiring another company that might have a different cloud vendor is also easier in this case.

Meeting data sovereignty

As your company grows, you might want to locate your data-processing operations within the regions you serve. Having a multi-cloud strategy gives you the flexibility to select the cloud that's strongest in each region, so you can set up an architecture that minimizes latency, upholds geo-residency requirements, and complies with data sovereignty mandates. You'll be able to expand your operation into remote regions without sacrificing access to data, and you'll discover the value of a single source of truth for your entire organization.

Data replication also makes sharing and monetizing data and bringing partners into an exchange easier, all while upholding the fundamental principle of data sharing: Data exists locally in a single source, from which it can be accessed rather than moved.

Simplifying security

When working with multiple clouds, how do you ensure the same security configurations and techniques apply to all of your cloud providers? Will you have to resolve differences in audit trails and event logs? Will your cybersecurity experts have to deal with different rule sets, or tinker with multiple key management systems to encrypt data? A unified code base spanning all cloud platforms simplifies all of these operations. You won't need to hire people with unique skillsets or maintain familiarity with the nuances of multiple clouds.

REMEMBER

Advanced replication technology allows you to easily share data among many regions and across different vendor clouds — without setting up data pipelines, copying data, or resolving differences in security. This broadens your markets, makes it easier to engage partners, and gives you a robust ecosystem for analyzing and sharing data.

Chapter **8**

Securing Your Data

The facts about cloud security: In most instances, your data is safer in the cloud than it is in your own data center. A 2019 survey of IT executives by Deloitte, authored by a team including Tom Davenport, Ashish Verma, and David Linthicum, found more than 90 percent of organizations primarily keep their data on cloud platforms. Data security and governance were the top drivers for organizations to migrate their data to the cloud, the survey found.

SaaS cloud providers serve thousands or even millions of custom-ers. They can afford the resources to provide industrial-strength, end-to-end data security. However, not all cloud providers put the effort into securing your data. Look closely, and you'll see security capabilities vary widely.

Exploring the Fundamentals

Protecting your data and complying with pertinent regulations must be fundamental to the architecture, implementation, and operation of a cloud data warehouse service. All aspects of the service must be centered on protecting your data as part of a multilayered security strategy that considers both current and evolving security threats. This strategy should address external interfaces, access control, data storage, and physical infrastructure in conjunction with comprehensive monitoring, alerts, and verifiable cybersecurity practices.

Encrypting data by default

Encrypting data means applying an encryption algorithm to translate the clear text into cipher text. This is fundamental to security. Encrypt data from the time it leaves your premises, through the Internet, and into the warehouse: when it's stored on disk, when it's moved into a staging location, when it's placed within a database object, and when it's cached within a virtual data warehouse. Query results should also be encrypted. All of this should be built in, not an option.

The vendor should also protect the decryption keys that decode your data. The best service providers employ AES 256-bit encryption with a hierarchical key model. This method encrypts the encryption keys and instigates key rotation that limits the time during which any single key can be used.

REMEMBER

Your data likely lives in many locations. You have to protect and control the data flow at each point. All data must be encrypted end-to-end and automatically, in transit and at rest.

Applying access control

Securing data is just one aspect of comprehensive security. Data breaches often result from users selecting weak passwords coupled with rudimentary authentication procedures. A cloud data warehouse service should always authorize users, authenticate credentials, and grant users access only to the data they're authorized to access.

The starting point is *role-based access control*, which ensures users can access only the data they're permitted to see. Access control should be applied to all database objects including tables, schemas, and any virtual extensions to the data warehouse. For maximum convenience and security, your cloud data warehouse should also provide *multifactor authentication*, which requires secondary verification such as a one-time security code sent to a user's mobile phone.

Single sign-on procedures and *federated authentication* make it easier for people to log in to the data warehouse service directly from other sanctioned applications. Federated authentication centralizes identity management and access control procedures, making it easier for your team to manage user access privileges.

Your cloud data warehouse vendor shouldn't have access to unencrypted customer data unless you explicitly grant that access.

Patching, updates, and network monitoring

Software patches and security updates must be installed on all pertinent software components as soon as those updates are available. The vendor should also deploy periodic security testing (also known as penetration testing) by an independent security firm to proactively check for vulnerabilities.

Physical security measures in the data center should include biometric access controls, armed guards, and video surveillance to ensure no one gains unauthorized access. All physical and virtual machines must be further controlled with rigorous software procedures for auditing, monitoring, and alerting. As an added protection, file integrity monitoring (FIM) tools ensure critical system files aren't tampered with, and IP address whitelists enable you to restrict access to the data warehouse to only trusted networks. (A whitelist is a list of email addresses or domain names from which an email blocking program will allow messages to be received.)

Security "events," generated by cybersecurity monitoring systems that watch over the network, should be automatically logged in a tamper-resistant security information and event management (SIEM) system. Automatic alerts should be sent to security personnel when suspicious activity is detected.

Ensuring data protection, retention, and redundancy

In case of a mishap, you should be able to instantly restore or query previous versions of your data in a table or database within a specified retention period, as governed by your service-level agreement (SLA) with the cloud data warehouse provider. A complete data-retention strategy should go beyond duplicating data within the same cloud region or zone: It should replicate that data among multiple availability zones for geographic redundancy. Optionally, automatic failover to these other zones can ensure continuous business operations.

Requiring tenant isolation

If your data warehouse vendor uses a multitenant cloud environment, in which many customers share the same physical infrastructure, make sure each customer has a virtual data warehouse isolated from all other data warehouses. For storage, this isolation should extend down to the virtual machine layer: Each customer's data storage environment should be isolated from every other customer's environment, governed by independent directories and unique encryption keys. Some vendors also offer dedicated virtual private networks (VPNs) and bridges from a customer's systems into the cloud data warehouse. These dedicated services ensure the most sensitive components of your data warehouse are completely separate from those of other customers.

Maintaining governance and compliance

Data governance ensures corporate data is properly accessed and used, and that day-to-day data management practices comply with all pertinent regulatory requirements. Governance policies establish rules and procedures to control the ownership and accessibility of your data. The types of information that commonly fall under these guidelines include credit card information, Social Security numbers, dates of birth, IP network information, and geolocation coordinates.

Demanding attestations and certifications

Compliance is not just about robust cybersecurity practices. It's also about ensuring your data warehouse provider can prove it has the required security procedures in place. Data breaches can cost millions of dollars to remedy and permanently damage relationships with your customers.

Industry-standard attestation reports verify cloud vendors use appropriate security controls. For example, a cloud data warehouse vendor needs to demonstrate it adequately monitors and responds to threats and security incidents and has sufficient incident response procedures in place (see Figure 8-1).

Industry-Standard Data Warehouse Security

Access
- Strong passwords
- IP whitelisting

Authentication
- Multifactor authentication
- Federated authentication

Authorization
- Role-based access control
- Data governance

Data
- End-to-end encryption
- Data replication

Infrastructure
- Physical security
- Isolated storage

FIGURE 8-1: Verify that all data traffic is encrypted and secure, and that your cloud providers hold all relevant certifications.

In addition to industry-standard technology certifications such as ISO/IEC 27001 and SOC 1/SOC 2 Type II, verify your cloud provider also complies with all applicable government and industry regulations. Depending on your business, this might include PCI, HIPAA/Health Information Trust Alliance (HITRUST), and FedRAMP certifications.

Ask for proof, and make sure your vendors provide a copy of the entire report for each pertinent standard, not just the cover letters. For example, the SOC 2 Type II report verifies that appropriate technical and administrative controls have been in place consistently for the last 12 months. The PCI-DSS attestation of compliance reveals whether your vendor properly stores and processes credit card information. If you handle protected health information, require that your vendors comply with HIPAA guidelines.

TIP

Compliance and attestations prove your data warehouse vendor is serious and transparent about security.

Cloud vendors should also supply evidence that third-party software vendors they work with are compliant and that they perform regular security audits. Your data is only as secure as the weakest link in the technology chain, so ensure all players have robust security controls in place and comply with industry-standard security practices. If any proof of compliance is missing, acquire supporting documentation.

Work only with cloud providers that demonstrate they uphold industry-sanctioned, end-to-end security practices, confirmed by independent auditors. These compliance considerations should comprise your minimum requirements for this important data repository.

Insisting on a Comprehensive Security Posture

Doing security well is expensive and requires specialized knowledge. Equipment failures, network breaches, and maintenance mishaps can result in data loss and introduce inconsistencies into your data. A comprehensive security practice encompasses many aspects. Your cloud data warehouse vendor should have procedures for safeguarding against accidental or intentional destruction. Some vendors provide rudimentary security capabilities, leaving encryption, access control, and security monitoring to you, the customer. Security should be a foundation of the data warehouse service; you shouldn't have to do anything extra to secure your data.

A vendor transparent about its security certifications is much more likely to have a solid security program.

Chapter 9

Minimizing Your Data Warehouse Costs

n this chapter, we examine how to run a cloud-built data warehouse and how your data warehouse vendor can help you minimize costs over the long term.

Minimizing the Cost of Storage

The more data you can store, the deeper the insights you can derive. Fortunately, cloud storage from Amazon, Microsoft, and Google has become relatively inexpensive, so you should not feel limited in the amount and types of data you store. Examine the terms to ensure your cloud data warehouse vendor isn't marking up these raw storage costs. The vendor should pass through the list prices direct to you. Your warehouse vendor can provide additional value by *compressing* your data threefold to fivefold. Threefold compression means you have one-third of the amount of data to store, at one-third the cost.

Examine terms of the usage agreement: You should have to pay only for storage you use, not for excess or "reserved" storage capacity. You also shouldn't pay to clone databases within your data warehouse for development and testing activities. You should be able to reference, not copy, your data multiple times and therefore not have to pay extra for storage.

Your cloud data warehouse should also allow you to store and query structured and semi-structured data such as JSON. Finally, look for a vendor that offers *multi-cloud capabilities*, because that can save future costs if you migrate your data warehouse to another cloud storage environment.

Maximizing Compute Efficiency

Compute resources are more expensive than storage resources, so your data warehouse service should allow you to scale each resource independently and make it easy to spin up exactly the compute resources you need under a usage-based pricing model. The vendor should bill you only for the resources you use — down to the second — and automatically suspend compute resources when you stop using them, to avoid runaway costs. Usage-based versus subscription-based pricing allows you to choose how you consume resources.

Flexible terms should also allow you to "right-size" your compute clusters to each workload. If you're running an extract, transfer, load (ETL) job with low compute requirements, you can match a small cluster to that workload rather than incur the cost of an overprovisioned cluster. If you need to test new machine learning modules, you can utilize a large cluster. This gives you fine-grained scalability for each workload while minimizing usage costs. Your warehouse will cost less to run than on-premises warehouses and their cloud-versioned cousins that crawl along, use huge resources, and produce limited results. Workloads will not slow, or even stall, thanks to compute clusters dedicated to each workload.

Chapter **10**

Six Steps to Getting Started with Cloud Data Warehousing

I n this chapter, we guide you through six key steps to choosing a cloud data warehouse for your organization. The process begins with evaluating your data warehouse needs and concludes with testing your top choice. By the end, you'll have a plan to help you choose your solution with confidence.

Step 1: Evaluate Your Needs

The data warehouse that's right for you should meet your current needs and be able to accommodate your future needs. Therefore, consider the nature of your data, the skills and tools already in place, your usage needs, the future plans for your business, and how a data warehouse can take your business further than you imagined:

>> **Data:** What types of data must the data warehouse contain? At what rate is new data created? How often will data move into the warehouse? What crucial data can't you access today?

>> **Fit with existing skills, tools, and processes:** What tools and skills from your team will apply to the various cloud data warehouse options? What processes will a cloud data warehouse impact?

>> **Usage:** Which users and applications will access the data warehouse? What types of queries will you run? How much data will users need to access, and how quickly? How will workloads vary over time? What performance do your users and applications require? How many users should access the data warehouse but don't today due to resource constraints?

>> **Data sharing:** Do you plan to securely share data across your organization and with customers and/or partners? If so, what types of data will you share, and will you create a data marketplace or exchange to also monetize data? Will you allow these data consumers to access raw data, or will you enrich that data by also offering data services such as analytics?

>> **Global access:** Do you plan to store data in a public object store, such as Amazon S3, Microsoft Azure, or Google Cloud Platform? Do you have specific functional, regional, or data sovereignty requirements that necessitate maintaining these relationships? Do you need a cross-cloud architecture to maximize regional deployment options, to bolster disaster recovery, or to ensure global business continuity?

>> **Resources:** What human resources are available to manage the data warehouse? How much investment do you wish to make to monitor and manage availability, performance, and security? Do you have focused expertise with data warehouse development and testing, or a DevOps team to streamline this?

Step 2: Migrate or Start Fresh

Every cloud data warehouse project should start with assessing how much of your existing environment should migrate to the new system and what should be built new for a cloud data warehouse. These decisions may address everything from design of the extract, transform, and load (ETL) processes to data models and software development lifecycle methods. Consider:

>> **Is this a brand-new project?** If so, it often makes sense to design the project to take full advantage of the capabilities of a cloud data warehouse rather than carry forward an existing implementation with constraints.

>> **Which parts of your current system cause the most headache?** A well-planned migration could focus on moving the most problematic workloads to the cloud data warehouse first. Or, you may want to migrate the more straightforward workloads to get quick wins.

>> **What aspects of your current system accommodate constraints no longer present with a cloud data warehouse?** Tools and processes designed to work around resource constraints, to avoid the disruptive effort required to add capacity, or to optimize cost may be unnecessary with the right cloud solution.

>> **How do current users and applications access the data warehouse?** Users and applications that rely on industry-standard interfaces, such as SQL, and use standard ETL and business intelligence tools, will experience less change adapting to a new approach.

>> **How are your data and analytics requirements likely to change in the future**? A solution built to evolve is likely to be around longer than expected and will reveal new opportunities that capitalize on advanced capabilities such as secure data sharing and global data access.

REMEMBER

If you have a large and complex traditional data warehouse, migrate a small part of the system to get comfortable with using a cloud data warehouse. Then you can iteratively expand your cloud footprint.

Step 3: Establish Success Criteria

How will you measure the success of moving to a new cloud data warehouse? Choose important business and technical requirements. Criteria should focus on performance, concurrency, simplicity, and total cost of ownership (TCO).

REMEMBER

If your new cloud data warehouse has capabilities not available in your previous system, and those capabilities are relevant to evaluating the business and technical success of your new solution, be sure to include them.

As you establish the success criteria of your new solution, determine how you'll measure that success by deciding which criteria are quantifiable and which are qualitative, how you'll measure the quantifiable criteria, and how you'll assess the qualitative criteria.

RESOLVING LATENCY ISSUES

CASE STUDY

White Ops is a leading provider of cybersecurity services. Unlike traditional approaches that employ statistical analysis, White Ops combats criminal activity by differentiating between robotic and human interaction, working to uncover and characterize new fraud patterns. This constant process requires storing and processing massive amounts of data.

White Ops had previously relied on NoSQL systems to store and process that data. However, the latency for results was at least 24 hours, depending on the workload. The more requests, the longer the delays.

To increase productivity and performance, White Ops implemented a cloud data warehouse with SQL as its core language and delivered as a service. The data warehouse enables White Ops to have all data in one place, scale elastically, query diverse data with standard SQL, and accelerate the evolution of its fraud prevention offerings.

White Ops can now consolidate and scale massive amounts of data, enable access to data without relying on specialists with deep programming skills, and help its customers avoid the devastating effects of online fraud.

Step 4: Evaluate Solutions

Once you determine your data warehouse needs and success criteria, you're ready to start evaluating solutions. Throughout this book, we detail the differences between available options (see Chapters 3, 4, and 5). As you compare, make sure they meet the following criteria:

>> Addresses current and future needs

>> Integrates structured and semi-structured data, stores it all in one place, and avoids creating data silos

>> Supports existing skills, tools, and expertise

>> Guards against data loss and enables easy data recovery

>> Secures your data with industry-standard password protection and encryption

- » Ensures data and analytics are always available
- » Streamlines the data pipeline so new data is available for analysis in the shortest possible amount of time
- » Optimizes time to value, so you can reap the benefits of your new data warehouse as soon as possible
- » Dedicates resources to isolated workloads
- » Shares data without having to copy or move live data and easily connects data providers and consumers
- » Replicates databases and keeps them synchronized across accounts, cloud platforms, and regions to improve business continuity and streamline expansion
- » Provides zero-copy database cloning for development and testing, and to support multiple use cases, such as reporting, data exploration, and predictive analytics
- » Makes it easy to recover lost data due to errors or attacks by rolling back to previous versions of data
- » Scales compute and storage independently and automatically, and scales concurrency without slowing performance

Step 5: Calculate TCO

If you choose a cloud data warehouse based on price, consider the TCO for a conventional data warehouse, which includes the cost of licensing, typically based on the number of users; hardware (servers, storage devices, networking); data center (office space, electricity, administration, maintenance, and ongoing management); data security (password protection and encryption); solutions to ensure availability and resiliency; support for scaling and concurrency; and creation of development and staging environments.

For some solutions, you might need to consider additional costs, such as building and managing multiple data marts, having multiple copies of data in different data marts, training people, having multiple systems (for example, SQL and NoSQL) to handle diverse data, and so on.

Calculating the costs of cloud data warehouse options is usually easier, but it varies according to the vendor's services. Assuming you outsource everything to the vendor by choosing a data-warehouse-as-a-service (DWaaS), you can calculate the TCO based on the monthly subscription fee. If you opt for an infrastructure-as-a-service (IaaS) or platform-as-a-service (PaaS) solution (see Chapter 5), you need to add the costs of whatever software, administration, and services the solution doesn't include.

TIP

Organizations typically calculate the TCO over the expected lifetime of the data warehouse, which is commonly one to three years. A key caveat: People often assume a cloud system runs 24/7 and at high capacity, overlooking the savings possible when a cloud solution is scaled up and down dynamically in response to changing demand, and only charges by the second.

Step 6: Set Up a Proof of Concept

After investigating different cloud data warehouse options, viewing demos, asking questions, and meeting with each vendor's team, do a proof of concept (PoC) before you choose. A PoC tests a solution to determine how well it serves your needs and meets your success criteria. Think of it as a test drive. It typically lasts a day or two, but it can be conducted over the course of several weeks. You request a PoC from a prospective vendor with the general understanding that if the solution performs satisfactorily, you'll buy the product. Or, in the case of cloud data warehousing, you'll subscribe to the service.

TIP

When setting up your PoC, list all requirements and success criteria — not just the issues you're trying to resolve, but everything possible with a cloud solution.

Develop a comprehensive checklist of data warehousing needs and your success criteria as a starting point. Make sure the new data warehouse does everything your current data warehouse does but better, and that it overcomes the drawbacks of the current system. If you do a PoC with multiple vendors, use the same checklist for each.